CITRUS COUNTRY

BY LYNN M. STONE

THE ROURKE CORPORATION, INC.
Vero Beach, FL 32964

Edited by Sandra A. Robinson

PHOTO CREDITS

All photos © Lynn M. Stone

ACKNOWLEDGMENTS

The author sincerely thanks the following organizations in citrus country for their kind and enthusiastic assistance in this project: Citrus World, Inc.; Three Gee Dee Company; Waverly Growers Cooperative; Florida Cattleman's Association

DEDICATION

For Kent Gooch, A Poor Orange Farmer

Library of Congress Cataloging-in-Publication Data
Stone, Lynn M.
Citrus country / by Lynn M. Stone.
    p.   cm. — (Back roads)
Includes index.
Summary: Gives a historical description of the areas in Florida where citrus fruits are grown and provides specific details on the cultivation of oranges there.
ISBN 0-86593-304-9
1. Citrus fruits—Florida—Juvenile literature. 2. Orange—Florida—Juvenile literature. [1. Citrus fruits—Florida. 2. Orange—Florida.] I. Title.
II. Series: Stone, Lynn M. Back roads.
SB369.2.F6S88 1993
338.1'7431'09759—dc20   93-22978
                                                                  CIP
                                                                   AC

TABLE OF CONTENTS

CHAPTER 1

CITRUS COUNTRY

Citrus. The word itself is as juicy as a Florida orange. That's appropriate – because oranges are citrus fruits. They are also the USA's single most valuable fruit, worth over a billion dollars each year. About 70 percent of America's homegrown oranges are picked from Florida trees, and nearly half of the state – a broad citrus belt of sorts – is citrus country.

About 30 Florida counties grow citrus **commercially,** for the marketplace. Those counties extend from Putnam in north central Florida, to Dade on the Florida peninsula's southern rim 300 miles away. The real heart of citrus country, though, is much more compact. It spreads roughly in a 60-mile radius from the town of Sebring in Highlands County. Stretch that distance a bit on the south and southeast, and the circle around Sebring gathers in the state's best citrus-producing counties: St. Lucie, Polk, Hendry, Indian River, Hardee, Highlands, DeSoto and Martin, in order of production.

Florida oranges, grapefruit and other citrus fruits, such as lemons, tangerines and limes, are raised in **groves.** A grove is a plantation or farm where fruit-bearing trees are planted, tended and picked. Florida citrus groves cover more than 800,000 acres. The overwhelming majority are

Three-quarters of the Florida orange juice crop is processed into sweet, tangy juice

Florida citrus groves, planted in neat, parallel rows, cover more than 800,000 acres and yield billions of pounds of fruit

planted with orange and grapefruit trees. These trees yield an annual fruit harvest that weighs billions of pounds – 12 1/2 billion pounds of oranges alone! Seventy-five percent of the fruit is converted into juice. Some of that juice and fresh fruit is exported, largely to Canada and Europe. Most of Florida's oranges and juice are gobbled up and gulped down in the United States.

The boundaries of citrus country have shifted southward in recent years in response to killing frosts. Orange and grapefruit trees are subtropical plants. They can thrive during periods of cool weather, but not in frigid weather. The Florida peninsula rarely has nights of prolonged temperatures below freezing, but it takes only *one* to batter a citrus grove.

Thousands of acres of citrus groves have been abandoned, north of an imaginary line from Tampa on the west coast to Melbourne on the east coast. Cold weather was the main culprit. A visitor to the 200-foot tall Citrus Tower in Clermont used to be able to gaze upon 17 million orange trees. It was as if the whole world were an orange grove. Today the Citrus Tower stands north of prime citrus country. About the only oranges around are in the gift shop. The view from the tower top now is of lakes and suburban housing developments. "We had hard freezes four years in a row in the early 1980s," an employee at the tower explained. "Everything north of Highway 50 was zapped. People were afraid to replant."

The rapid growth of certain cities – Orlando, for one – has also helped push the citrus industry further south. The citrus industry in Orange County, for example, has suffered from freezes. It has also been nibbled away by a growing Orlando. Despite its name, Orange County ranks only 20th among Florida counties in citrus production. New groves, especially in Collier and Hendry Counties in southwest Florida, have replaced the loss of northern groves.

Most of the orange groves in citrus country are on flat land. Like a huge, basking lizard, the Florida peninsula as a whole lies snug to the level of the seas that surround it. The elevated groves of Florida's central ridge are the exceptions. The ridge is one of the citrus country's traditional centers of orange and grapefruit production. The ridge is Florida's divide, the lizard's spine – a low, sandy rise that extends about 100 miles from south of Leesburg to Sebring. The "peaks" of the central ridge are about 250 feet above sea level – the distance a strong-armed quarterback can fire a football. That kind of altitude doesn't make anyone's ears pop. Nevertheless,

Citrus groves thrive where they are safe from killing frosts

Floridians long ago decided that the "high country" of the ridge would be their Colorado. With a keen sense of exaggeration, they named communities in the region Mount Dora, Mount Plymouth and Mount Homer. Another lump of hard sand was christened Iron Mountain.

Still, a person can stand on the ridge and have a panoramic view of the countryside. On a clear day you can't see forever, but as a native of the region said, "On a clear day you can probably see across the lake." You can also see the ground gently slouch away to the east and to

Citrus trees prosper on the "heights" of central Florida's sandy ridge, the state's "spine" between Leesburg and Sebring

the west from the ridge. Water that drains from the west slope runs to the Gulf of Mexico. The east slope drains to the Atlantic.

From almost anywhere along the southern half of the ridge, the land is green with row upon row of citrus. Here the world truly is an orange grove. The ridge soil, sandy and fast-draining, is ideal for the roots of orange and grapefruit trees. They approve of moisture, but not wet feet. In the spring, Valencia oranges cling to the trees and mingle with white orange blossoms. It's a special time of year on the ridge. If one feels dizzy, it's not the altitude causing the sensation. Instead, it's the sweet orange blossom fragrance, swept by a mountain – er, ridge – breeze.

The groves of citrus country are planted in unfailingly neat, parallel rows of trees. Without their fruit, the grapefruit trees look very much like the orange and tangerine trees.

The foliage of grapefruit trees tends to be lighter green than the deep, waxy green of orange and tangerine trees. The trees are much easier to tell apart in October when the first heavy fruits bend their branches.

Many of the most robust grove trees stand 15 to 30 feet tall. Citrus trees can grow to greater heights, but they are regularly **pruned,** or trimmed, by growers. Some trees are also pruned by frost. Groves usually have trees of several sizes, each size occupying a portion of the grove.

From just the right place, a person can see one or more of the thousands of polka dot lakes that shimmer throughout central Florida. Most of them formed from

Orange blossoms bloom in spring and spice the breeze with a sweet fragrance

sinkholes, a common and curious feature of citrus country. Sinkholes occur because of the limestone deposits under the topsoil. Limestone is **porous;** it contains holes and chambers through which water passes and settles. Over time, the action of underground water can cause the ceiling of a limestone chamber – a cave – to collapse. When the cave ceiling gives way near the surface, a sinkhole appears. The largest sinkholes become lakes.

The sweep of citrus country takes in thousands of square miles of central Florida. In the cities and towns of the region, and throughout peninsular Florida, population growth is a way of life. Most of the residents in citrus country don't speak with a **Dixie dialect.** Yet, in comparison to Florida's coastal communities, central Florida still has a fair share of **natives,** the true Florida **Crackers.** No one is quite sure of the origin of the word *Cracker.* It may have been coined at the time pioneer horse, mule and cattle drivers were cracking their braided rawhide whips. In any case, Florida Crackers are still fixtures in citrus country.

If central Florida is a stronghold for the first-born of its pioneer stock, it is also a stronghold for some of its first products – citrus, cattle and phosphate. Citrus country is not just the unending lines of manicured trees that it appears to be. Citrus country back roads lead through a landscape mixed with citrus, woodland, and pastures

Ripe for picking, Valencia oranges share the branches with blossoms – the beginning of next year's Valencia crop

Irrigation lines snake through a new grove in citrus country

cultivated and wild. Okeechobee County, for example, produces a whopping amount of citrus. Yet it is also the state's largest producer of dairy cattle. The region, however, is much better known for its beef herds. Throughout the heart of citrus country, beef cattle graze on prairies that sometimes step right up to a citrus grove.

Central Florida has a long tradition of raising beef cattle on its broad, grassy plains. Ponce de Leon brought Spanish cattle to Florida in 1521. During the Civil War (1861-1865), salted beef from Florida helped feed Confederate soldiers of the South. It probably fed more than a few **Yankees,** too. Florida is the nation's 16th ranking state in overall cattle production.

Egrets fly over a herd of Holstein dairy cattle in citrus country

Many of the beef cattle on Florida ranches are lean, wild-looking creatures. Ranchers also produce purebred Brahman cattle, the gray, humpbacked breed specifically developed to withstand hot, humid weather.

Phosphate mines are part of the landscape, too. Phosphate rock is **quarried,** or dug, from the ground and used primarily for fertilizer. Florida is the nation's largest producer of phosphate, and much of it is mined in citrus country.

Central Florida raised beef cattle, like this Brahman bull, long before it raised citrus products. The cattle egret following the bull will snap up insects that the bull disturbs as it tromps through the pasture. Cattle

egrets, now common in central Florida, were unknown in the state until 1952 when they spread northward from British Guiana.

An air view of one of central Florida's phosphate pits from which

phosphate rock is mined and processed into fertilizers

FLORIDA

Pensacola

Tallahassee
Panama City

Jacksonville

St. Augustine

Gainesville

ATLANTIC OCEAN

Leesburg

Kennedy
Space
Center

Orlando

Clermont

Merritt Island

Melbourne

Kissimmee
State Park

Tampa

St. Petersburg

Highlands Hammock
State Park

Fort
Pierce

Okeechobee

Sarasota

Sebring
Myakka River
State Park

Lake
Okeechobee

Hobe
Sound

Punta Gorda

Palm
Beach

Fort Myers

Fort
Lauderdale

GULF OF MEXICO

Naples

Miami

FLORIDA KEYS

CITRUS COUNTRY

Some of the most interesting back roads in citrus country meander past tracts of old Florida wilderness. Some of its snarls and tangled swamps are fairly well-protected on the vast beef ranches. State parks and reserves also protect segments of the original Florida. There are blackwater rivers and creeks that course through bottomland forests where otters, alligators and crow-sized pileated woodpeckers live. There are wide prairies, wet and dry, with their marshes of cattails and purple pickerel-weed, homes for sandhill cranes and dozens of other long-legged waterbirds. There are clumps of pine and cabbage palms, fragments of scrub forest, and swamps of ancient baldcypress, the trees with "knees."

As any ranch hand will tell you, citrus country has not been entirely manicured.

CHAPTER 2

THE FIRST CITRUS GROVES

Oranges are no more native, or original, to Florida than armadillos. Armadillos, the armor-plated ant eaters, also live in abundance in citrus country. It just happens that Florida's warm weather and open spaces are as appealing to alien animals as they are to Yankees and other alien people. The armadillo, walking catfish, Cuban treefrog and Bahama anole are just a few of the critters who have – uninvited – taken up housekeeping in Florida. The plant list of unwanted immigrants is much longer and uglier, with Australian pines and Brazilian peppers at the top of the list. Fortunately, not all aliens are pests. Consider, for instance, the orange tree.

Florida orange trees are not native, but their roots in Florida go back nearly 500 years. And unlike pest plants, oranges don't take over the landscape unless someone wants them to. The first oranges in Florida probably arrived with Ponce de Leon in 1513. Ponce de Leon "discovered" Florida and set the stage for a series of explorations. The Spaniards brought oranges with them from home, where oranges were no more unusual than bulls. Undoubtedly, seeds from those Spanish oranges resulted in Florida's first orange trees.

Florida's first grapefruit grove was established by a Frenchman, Count Odet Phillippe, near Tampa in 1823, but grapefruit was not a commercial success in Florida until the late 1800s

A grove of citrus bathes in sunlight just a few miles west of the Indian River near Fort Pierce

Florida was the object of international haggling and brawling for the next 300 years. At one time or another the Spanish, French, English, Americans and assorted Native Americans clashed over the territory before it became a state in 1845. However, the prospect of raising oranges in this sun-drenched wilderness was not high on anyone's list of "Things I Must Do Today." Then in 1776 along came Jesse Fish, an enterprising New Yorker with a taste for citrus and cash. Mr. Fish grew oranges in a grove on an island off St. Augustine, high on Florida's Atlantic coast. He shipped his fruit to London and made a good living.

The commercial marketing of Florida oranges didn't really start, however, until after Florida became U.S. property in 1821. Most planting was in the St. Augustine area. Growers there in 1834 shipped 2 1/2 million oranges north. The fledgling citrus industry was in for a shivering shock though. On February 8, 1835, Arctic air blasted

Florida. The temperature dipped to 11° in St. Augustine. It might have been a choice time to replace orange trees with hockey sticks. The orange industry was almost dead.

One grove, tucked away on Merritt Island, where the Kennedy Space Center rises today, escaped the freeze. That was the grove of Douglas Dummett, a Connecticut Yankee who had moved to Florida and planted orange trees in 1830. From Mr. Dummett's trees, Florida's citrus groves were replanted.

Dummett's grove was the first in the Indian River region, which soon became famous for its citrus. The Indian River is really not a river, but a sea lagoon. One hundred and twenty miles long and two miles wide in many places, the Indian River lies between the mainland and a chain of narrow barrier islands on Florida's Atlantic coast. In 1842, Captain Mills Olcott Burnham, a former Vermonter, led a group south from Merritt Island and established a community near present-day Fort Pierce. Burnham's travels led to new Indian River groves.

After the Civil War, most would-be orange growers settled along the St. Johns River near Jacksonville. Others planted near Orlando and a few straggled into the Indian River country. Jacksonville was especially attractive because it had a major shipping port. But it was also in the northeast part of Florida. In December, 1894, and February, 1895, two cold fronts swept into northern Florida. The first freeze crippled the trees and the second freeze killed them. Florida's growing citrus industry had shipped 5 million boxes of oranges north in 1894. The year after the freeze, the state shipped 147,000 boxes. The groves in the Jacksonville-St. Augustine area were forever

abandoned. Growers in the Orlando area and along the central ridge regrouped and gradually re-established their groves.

Meanwhile, citrus farming along the Indian River developed quickly in the 1890s. Henry M. Flagler planted his Florida East Coast Railroad tracks along the entire length of the river, from Titusville to Hobe Sound. By the 1920s, conveniently served by the railroad, Indian River fruit had become internationally known and desired. Even today, Indian River citrus enjoys a reputation for being Florida's sweetest and juiciest.

Florida's citrus industry continued to grow with the state. In 1942, Florida passed California in orange production. In the next 50 years it became the increasingly dominant U.S. citrus producer, although not without concerns.

One bright day in early December, a modern-day citrus grove owner in Plant City discussed some of those concerns. He said there was always the possibility of a killing frost, especially in the northern counties like his own, Hillsborough. He'd seen grove owners walk around with glazed eyes after nature had dealt them a hard freeze. Farming oranges, he said, was like owning stock. No guarantees. Then there was the negative impact that other orange-producing nations, like Egypt and Mexico, might have on citrus prices in Florida.

*A citrus country orange
grower pauses to sample the
juice from one of his oranges*

But on a bright winter's day that feels like summer, why worry? The grower left his office and hiked into his grove. "You know," he said, "you do yourself a disservice if you don't stop once in awhile to enjoy it." The early fruit was full and ripe. The grove owner, his hired hands and nature had performed well. The owner swiped an orange from a tree. He peeled it halfway down with a knife. "Remember," he said, "California oranges are beautiful, but Florida oranges have juice in them."

He bit into the fruit, which fairly exploded – an orange water balloon filled with juice. Juice trickled down his chin. A Californian would have warned him: "Don't ever try that without a bathing suit on!" He spit a couple of seeds on the ground, an old Florida custom. The Spaniards were doing the same thing nearly 500 years ago. He paused and shifted his eyes to the rows of green leaves and golden fruit. "Nobody pays orange growers anything for pretty trees," he had said. But now, looking down the rows, he remembered why he loved the citrus business.

CHAPTER 3

ORANGES

Truth is, if those seeds on the ground were to sprout, they would be plucked up like weeds. Citrus trees raised for fruit aren't grown from seeds. An orange tree will grow from an orange seed, but no one will like it. It is thorny and may take 15 years to bear fruit that is, at best, so-so. Instead, growers **graft** a section of orange tree to the **rootstock** of another type of citrus, such as a lemon. The upper frame of the tree grows to be an orange tree. It is basically thornless. With expert care, it will bear fruit in three or four years, and it will produce more fruit and sweeter fruit than a seeded tree. In addition, its rootstock can be hand-picked to do well in the soil and climate where it will be planted.

Most orange trees are now grafted to the rootstock of a citrus known as Carrizo. Sour orange, a rootstock traditionally used in Indian River groves, has been credited with that region's particularly sweet and juicy oranges.

Grafting is performed by cutting a small leaf stalk from an orange or grapefruit tree. One end of the stalk is fitted under the trunk bark of the little host tree, the Carrizo, for example, which is no thicker than a pen. The planter wraps the graft, the joint where the leaf stalk has been fitted. After six months or a year, the orange tree has bloomed on its borrowed roots, and it

By placing a styrofoam jacket around a young tree, growers reduce the chance of damage from ants and other citrus enemies

can be planted in the grove. With luck, it will produce fruit for 50 years or more.

Citrus trees have as many enemies as Superman, although a different cast of characters – ants, sucking scale insects, heart rot, foot rot, young tree decline, rust mites, lightning and cold weather, to name a few. A successful grove owner taps a battery of defenses to keep the citrus trees green and giving. Basically, the orange grove owner's arsenal consists of mechanical cultivation, **insecticides** to kill and control insects, **herbicides** to control weeds, and various fertilizers. Modern spraying devices – micro-jets – serve three purposes: They irrigate trees in the dry season. They can be activated to spray a warmer-than-air mist in cold weather. They can also be used to apply liquid fertilizer.

The ideal mix of sunshine, soil, temperatures and rainfall makes citrus country oranges swell with juice

Despite being subject to viruses, funguses, insects and cold, citrus are quite hardy. They tolerate Florida's heat and the cycle of wet and dry seasons. They can grow in poor-quality, sandy soil. The combination of about 52 inches of rain per year, generally warm days and cool winter nights is a magic wand for Florida citrus. The state's grapefruit and oranges are the world's juiciest.

Growers plant several varieties of citrus. Each has its advantages. Hamlin and navel oranges, for example, ripen early. That makes them more likely to avoid freezes. Valencia oranges, which make up about half the Florida orange crop, ripen late, but they have the most juice. Each variety of citrus has taste and color qualities that are both peculiar to the variety and to its grove location. Hamlins are deliciously sweet, but their pale yellow juice doesn't look like traditional orange juice. A Valencia on the central ridge will not taste exactly like a Valencia grown in an Indian River grove. And a Florida orange tree transplanted to California will bear more beautiful, but less juicy, oranges.

Whether they are in Spain, California, Florida or another place, orange and grapefruit trees belong to the citrus group of the rue family of plants. Citrus trees and shrubs typically have thorns and firm, edible fruit. Citrus fruits usually have thick rinds, or peels, and pulpy, juicy flesh.

Oranges and grapefruit are classified as berries by **horticulturists,** the people who experiment with and grow new varieties of plants. Berries include fleshy fruits that often have several seeds. Even seedless varieties of citrus have a few seeds. Grapes and melons are berries, too.

Horticulturists continually work to develop new citrus. Whatever they produce will no doubt continue to be full of vitamin C, with a healthy dash of vitamin A and several B vitamins.

CHAPTER 4

FROM BRANCH TO BOX AND BOTTLE

The secret to finding goodness in oranges is knowing when to pick them. Americans have never been colorblind in regard to oranges. Oranges have to be *orange,* or they are ignored. The blood oranges, popular in Spain, are tasty and grow well in Florida, but they are too *red.* The problem with Hamlin juice, until it's blended with more conventional juice, is that it is too *yellow.* Americans don't buy green oranges either, but growers know that green and greenish oranges may be ripe and ready. An orange is ready for picking when its sugar and juice content reach a certain high level, and its acid content decreases. The greenish peel does not affect the orange's taste or juice.

Florida has experimented with mechanical orange pickers. The state's growers have used shakers, wind machines and water guns. Robots may be next. Meanwhile, about 90 percent of Florida oranges are hand-picked. The most successful pickers have great tolerance for hard work. Their income is based on the number of field boxes they can fill during a day's work. A field box holds 90 pounds of oranges. The best pickers can fill 80 or 100 boxes. A picker who fills 100 boxes picks about 20,000 oranges.

Picking oranges requires agility, stamina and knowing how to place a ladder in the tree

The picker works from a ladder and drops oranges into a large shoulder bag. A full bag weighs about 45 pounds. A picker prefers trees that are loaded with fruit. The average tree holds 1,500 oranges. Occasionally trees have 8,000 to 10,000 oranges, the kind of trees that chimpanzees dream about.

Oranges are trucked to either a packinghouse or juice plant. Packinghouses sort oranges according to size and grade. Workers wash and lightly wax the oranges. When necessary, the packinghouse applies an orange dye to green oranges to make them more attractive to buyers. The oranges are packaged in bags or cartons and distributed for gift fruit or fresh fruit sales.

Packinghouse oranges that are bruised, but otherwise unhurt, are trucked to a juice plant, or cannery. That, of course, is where three-quarters of the orange crop goes

Oranges arrive at juice plants and packinghouses by the truckload

Conveyors transport oranges through washers and into a plant where the juice will be extracted and processed

anyway. With their tall loops of pipe, juice plants look like they could refine oil. Their smell, however, is strictly of oranges. Machines extract juice from oranges, and other machines later **pasteurize** it. Pasteurization is a heat process that kills harmful bacteria. After pasteurization, the juice is piped to cans, bottles and cartons. Juice plants also produce orange juice **concentrate,** in which the juice solids are separated from water. The concentrate can be frozen and canned, or later blended with water and sold as "100% Pure Unsweetened Orange Juice from Concentrate."

Orange peels, seeds and pulp have a variety of commercial uses. Processed peels are a major source of cattle feed. The oil of peels is an ingredient in some paints, baking mixes and perfumes.

In a citrus packinghouse, workers sort oranges moving by on a conveyer line, according to size and quality

Packinghouses and juice plants are marvelously complex and efficient operations. Company inspectors and U.S. Government inspectors work together to insure that food products being packaged meet high standards of nutrition and cleanliness.

The end of the line: oranges are packed in boxes for shipping

CHAPTER 5

FLORIDA SCRUB

Wherever farmland exists, a person might well wonder, "What covered that land before people changed it into farmland?" Some of the farmland in citrus country groves was once Florida scrub. Florida scrub is a special kind of woodland. With a little know-how, a person traveling through the citrus country can still find patches of scrub.

Scrub is one of the most unique natural communities of plants and animals in citrus country. Scrub has dense thickets of woody shrubs and broad patches of white sand. Lacy, little pillows of a curious plant called lichen grow on the sandy ground. The scrub may have scattered sand pines or small, spidery oaks. The scrub looks like a shrub forest that can't grow up – which is exactly what it is. Scrub plants remain low to the ground because the soil is nearly pure sand. The soils lack the **nutrients,** or nourishing contents, of other woodland soils. Water is another problem for scrub life. Plenty of rain pelts the scrub, but the sand does a poor job of trapping and holding it. The result is an almost desertlike environment for the plants and animals of scrub. Each member of the community has had to find particular ways – **adaptations** – to make rapid use of water. The scrub oak has adapted with shallow, wide-ranging roots.

Many of the scrub plants are **endemics,** which means that they are found only in one particular region and nowhere else. Several of the endemics, such as the scrub

Florida's scrub is a natural habitat that has disappeared in much of citrus country

lupine and scrub blazing star, are **endangered.** They are in danger of extinction.

The wild animals of the scrub are generally secretive. Many of them live in or near the ground. Rustling in a pocket of fallen leaves may be the only clue that a scrub animal is nearby. The blue-tailed mole skink is a lizard of some scrub. It is a rustler, much easier to hear than to see. Another rustler is the rufous-sided towhee, a bright-eyed songbird that scratches among the leaves.

The gopher tortoise lives in burrows in the scrub lands. It has powerful forelimbs and stubby claws for digging. The silky, blue-black indigo snake also lives in the scrub, along with bobcats and occasional deer.

The member of the scrub community best-known to residents of citrus country is the scrub jay. This attractive relative of the blue jay wears blue and gray feathers with black trim. Wild scrub jays become quite tame. They take handouts of peanuts and sunflower seeds from their human neighbors.

The thickets, snarls and desertlike conditions of the Florida scrub are home for the scrub jay

Two-thirds of the Florida scrub has been bulldozed away and converted to homes, stores, parking lots and citrus groves. Along the central ridge about 90 percent of the scrub has vanished. Scrub lands are prized by developers because they are well-drained. Visitors to citrus country can prowl Florida scrub at Highlands Hammock State Park in Sebring.

CHAPTER 6

VISITING CITRUS COUNTRY

Using the 60-mile radius of Sebring as a guide, visitors to citrus country will find a remarkable variety of attractions, natural and otherwise. Disney World at Lake Buena Vista, Cypress Gardens at Winter Haven, the Bok Tower Gardens at Lake Wales, and the Arcadia Rodeo are sure bets.

Roadside citrus stands are seeded throughout central Florida. They are excellent sources of cold, freshly-squeezed orange juice, fresh fruit and citrus jellies, and orange blossom honey, the handiwork of local bees. Many of the stands by groves will let you pick you own citrus. If you'd like to visit a fruit packinghouse, contact the Florida Department of Citrus in Lakeland for a list of packinghouses and groves that offer tours.

Several state parks in citrus country reveal Florida as it was a century or two ago. One of the most unique is 5,000-acre Lake Kissimmee State Park, 15 miles east of Lake Wales, on the shores of Lakes Kissimmee, Tiger and Rosalie. Kissimmee – be sure to accent the second syllable – has a weekend living history production that re-creates the life of a Florida ranch camp in the 1870s. A captive herd of rare, long-horned scrub cattle enhance the program.

Nearly as tall as a man, sandhill cranes prowl the shores of many citrus country lakes and prairies in a search for frogs, snakes, salamanders and aquatic animals

42

Citrus country lakes lure fishermen

The park has 13 miles of hiking trails, an observation tower, and vistas of marsh, prairie and lakeshore. It is a likely place to see bald eagles, Florida sandhill cranes, snail kites (a type of hawk) and 150 other species of birds.

Another 28,000 acres of natural Florida is on display at Myakka River State Park, 50 miles west of Sebring near Sarasota. Fishermen cast for bass and bream in Upper and Lower Myakka Lake, competing with ospreys, bald eagles and great blue herons. Most fishermen report that the Myakka lakes have more alligators than fish. But citrus country is swimming in lakes. You can probably find one with more fish than gators.

Variety in citrus country is not limited to your choice of orange!

GLOSSARY

adaptation - a special characteristic that enables a plant or animal to better survive in its particular habitat

commercial - relating to business and profit-making

concentrate - juice solids after the liquid content has been reduced

Cracker - a native resident of Florida or Georgia

dialect - a regional variety of language distinguished by its vocabulary, pronunciation and use of grammar

Dixie - referring to the South, the states below the Mason-Dixon line

endangered - in danger of extinction

endemic - a plant or animal that is found only in a particular region

graft - to attach a living part of a plant to the rootstock of another; the point of union

grove - a farm or plantation on which citrus is raised

herbicide - a chemical agent used to control and destroy certain plants

horticulturist - one who grows fruits, vegetables, flowers and ornamental plants

insecticide - a chemical agent used to control and destroy insects

native - original, or natural, to an area

nutrient - a substance providing an organism with nourishment

GLOSSARY

pasteurize – to heat at high temperature to destroy harmful organisms

porous – containing chambers or pores

prune – to cut back or trim for more productive growth

quarry – to dig or take from the ground

rootstock – a section of tree, including the roots, that is used for grafting

sinkhole – a cave-in or pit that results from the collapse of a limestone cavern ceiling

Yankee – people from the North, especially the New England states

INDEX

INDEX